9780434951277

Composers and their World

SCHUBERT

Schubert in 1821, aged 24.

Composers and their World

SCHUBERT

Kenneth and Valerie McLeish

HEINEMANN: LONDON

William Heinemann Ltd
15 Queen Street, Mayfair, London W1X 8BE
LONDON MELBOURNE TORONTO
JOHANNESBURG AUCKLAND

First published in 1979
© Kenneth and Valerie McLeish 1979

434 95127 7

Printed and bound in Great Britain
by W & J Mackay Limited, Chatham

Contents

Growing up

By the age of eight, some children already show musical genius. By Mozart's eighth birthday, for example, he was famous in a dozen countries. His tours as a child prodigy, composing and playing the harpsichord, were extremely successful, and he had appeared before almost every king, queen and prince in Europe.

Compared with such dazzling success, Schubert's musical ability as a child was much more ordinary. Looking at him at the age of eight, you might have said he had talent, especially for singing, but nothing remotely like Mozart's genius. These comments, written by his father after his death, suggest that he had ability—but no more than any other gifted child musician:

> Before he was five, I prepared him for elementary instruction, and in his sixth year sent him to school, where he was always higher in class than his fellow-scholars. When he was eight, I gave him preliminary instruction in violin playing and proceeded far enough with him to enable him to play duets fairly well. Then I sent him for singing lessons to Michael Holzer, the local choirmaster. Holzer often assured me, with tears in his eyes, that he had never had such a pupil.

1

"Whenever I set out to teach him something new," he said, "I find that he knows it already. In the end I did not give him any real instruction, but only listened to him in silent amazement."

The yard and entrance of the Imperial Seminary, where Schubert was a pupil.

Schubert's father, a schoolteacher, was a poor man. Schubert was the youngest of five children. There was no money to spare on school-fees—and in those days to get a good education you had to pay. Schubert's father decided to enter his son for a scholarship, to see if the singing ability which caused "silent amazement" in the local choirmaster also impressed more eminent musicians. On 30 September 1808 Schubert, aged eleven, went for an audition at the Imperial Seminary in Vienna, a famous choir school connected with the Imperial Chapel, and one of the best schools in Vienna. He passed the audition, and was given a scholarship.

SCHOOL

No one thought yet that Schubert would ever make music his profession. In fact his father intended him to become a teacher, like his two elder brothers. His lessons at the Seminary included other subjects as well as the singing, piano, violin and harmony that every choirboy learned. His school report when he was fifteen shows the main subjects he studied—and also that he was by no means a dunce:

Name: Schubert, Franz
Age: 15
Country, birthplace, domicile: Austria, Vienna, Imperial
   Seminary
Name and occupation of parent: Franz, schoolmaster
Behaviour: 1
Effort: 1
Religious instruction: 1

Latin: 2
Maths: 1
Geography and History: 1
Greek: 1
Remarks: none

Even so, once he moved away from Holzer, and began to mix with more eminent musicians, it soon became clear that Schubert's real talent was, after all, for music. On 26 September 1810 when he was thirteen, two years after he had entered the school, instructions were sent to the overseer of the Court music, that

> . . . especial attention is to be paid to the musical education of Franz Schubert, since he shows so excellent a talent for the art of music.

There were opportunities at school for all kinds of music-making. The choir performed in all the services of the Imperial Chapel, every Sunday and saint's day throughout the year. There were practice rooms with pianos (a rare thing in schools at this time) and a school orchestra good enough not just for straight-forward music, but also for difficult, "modern" works by Haydn, Mozart and Beethoven. Schubert became leader of this orchestra (playing the violin), and sometimes conducted it. Some of his earliest orchestral compositions, overtures, dances, even his first symphony, were first performed at school.

There was plenty of music at home, too. In particular, Schubert's singing delighted his family, and he probably wrote many songs for performance at family music-making. He played the viola in a string quartet (with his older brothers playing the two violins and his father the cello), and some of his earliest quartets were written for it. He went to concerts and the opera with his school-friends, and heard some of the finest music of the time, including the latest works of Beethoven, whom he much admired.

SCHOOLTEACHING

None the less, both he and his father still thought of music as a hobby, not a profession. When he was sixteen his voice broke, and he had to leave the choir. The school agreed to keep him on, providing he spent the summer holiday improving his non-musical subjects. But he left, and—perhaps to avoid doing

A view of the Danube and the city walls of Vienna (on the right). This drawing was made in 1821.

military service, from which schoolteachers were exempt—went straight to teacher training college. After this, he spent several years as an apprentice teacher in his father's school.

By all accounts, Schubert was a hopeless teacher. He seems to have found the lessons boring, and the pupils' bad behaviour a real trial. His sister later said of him that "he kept his hands busy on the children's ears"; there is a story that he was sacked for boxing the ears of a particularly stupid girl.

Part of the trouble may have been Schubert's size and appearance. By now he was fully grown, but he was only four feet eleven inches tall. He was chubby, and wore round, owlish glasses. He suffered from a weak chest and chronic indigestion. And even worse, from the classroom point of view, was his manner. His mind was on music, not children. On 16 October 1814, when he was seventeen, his first public success came with the performance of his *Mass in F*. In the next twelve months he wrote two more large-scale masses, two symphonies, four or five short operatic works, and over a hundred and fifty songs. If you work out the time it takes to fill even a single page with music, you can see that he must have had little "spare" time to concentrate on his pupils.

Finally Schubert gave schoolteaching up as a bad job, and set out to make a living as a professional musician. In this, apart from the difficulty of making enough money, there were other obstacles to overcome. Whatever his family and friends thought of his music, it was by no means to everyone's taste. On one occasion, when he was twenty, a copy of his song "The Erlking" (now regarded as one of his finest works) was rejected by the publishers, and sent back by mistake not to our Schubert, but to another Franz Schubert, an older, better-known composer. He sent the publishers a short, sharp reply:

6

... You enclosed the manuscript of Goethe's "Erlking" alleged to have been set by me. With the greatest astonishment I beg to state that this cantata was never composed by me. I shall retain the same in my possession in order to learn, if possible, who sent you that sort of trash in such an impolite manner, and also to discover the fellow who has thus misused my name.

This view of Vienna shows the city as it was in Schubert's boyhood. The fields and woods were among his favourite walking-places, all his life.

Two of Schubert's finest early compositions, and the best to begin with, are the songs "Gretchen at the Spinning-wheel" (*Gretchen am Spinnrade*) and "The Erlking" (*Der Erlkönig*). It is worth finding a translation of the words, to see Schubert's musical skill in "characterising" the people in the songs. Next, try some of the short string quartets written for family performance. They are shorter than the three later quartets, and several will be grouped on the same record. For larger works, begin with the two *Overtures in the Italian Style*, and move on to the *Symphony No 2 in B flat*.

Making a living

Being a composer ought to be a full-time job on its own. Apart from the nervous energy needed to invent the music in the first place, it takes a great deal of time and effort to write the notes down on paper, copy parts, send them off, perhaps even rehearse and perform the finished product. Unfortunately for composers, however, only a very few are able to live on the money their compositions earn. The others have to find an income from some-where else. Even today, most composers have other work: publishing, broadcasting, teaching or performing, for example. In Schubert's time, unless you had rich patrons, a second job of this kind was essential.

Schubert had found it hard to combine composing and school-teaching. But certainly he had to do *something*: he had no money of his own, and his father was too poor to support him. The problem was to find the best way to earn a living without taking too much valuable time from composing.

Several times in his life, he thought that the answer might be to take a job teaching music. In April 1816, when he was nineteen, he applied to become head teacher of the music academy at Laibach. He was turned down. The same thing happened ten years later in 1826: he applied for the post of assistant musical director at the Imperial Court, and was turned down. At other times his friends recommended him for musical jobs, but nothing ever came of them. Only twice did he get a position of this kind, and each time was with the same family, the Esterhazys, who had been Haydn's patrons years before. He spent the summers of 1818 and 1824 at the Esterhazy summer home, tutoring their children in music.

But two summer jobs are hardly a lifetime's career. Certainly Schubert never seems to have enjoyed teaching or settled down to it, even when it was connected with music. When he was twenty-two, his father wrote a letter to the authorities, begging them to give Schubert back his job in school:

> The undersigned therefore begs most obediently that his son Franz Schubert, who a year ago interrupted his school service ... in order to develop an artistic talent recognised by experts, may again be graciously confirmed as sixth assistant at his school ...

But the letter was never delivered. It seems that Schubert's ideas about his future were very different from his father's.

Another way of making money from music was to please audiences, and earn fees from concerts or opera performances. Schubert had ambitions to write for the theatre, and composed several stage works, ranging from incidental music for plays to full-length operas. Unfortunately neither critics nor audiences shared his taste in plays and stories, and his stage works were seldom given more than a few performances. Reviews like this one were common: it comes from a Leipzig paper of 29 August 1820, and deals with a "magic play" with music by Schubert called *The Magic Harp*:

> The score shows talent here and there; but on the whole it lacks technical resource and wants the grasp which only experience can give. Most of it is much too long, ineffective and fatiguing, the harmonic progressions are too harsh, the orchestration redundant, the choruses dull and feeble.

Another reviewer complained that Schubert "interrupted the words too often with music". Critics are often wrong, and the works they dislike turn out later to be masterpieces. But audiences tend to go by what they say, and a show with bad reviews finds it hard to survive. None of Schubert's stage works had any success, though the music was often excellent, and some of it (like the overture to *Rosamunde*) is nowadays well-known and regularly performed.

He had as little luck in the concert-hall, despite some successes in his teens. Only one really successful concert is known, a performance in 1828 which brought him in the huge sum of 800 gulden (a quarter of his whole year's income). The public preferred his songs and chamber works; orchestral musicians often

reacted to his music like the members of the Vienna Philharmonic
Orchestra, who tried over his Symphony No 9, but refused to
play it because they found it too long and too difficult.

WRITING FOR MONEY

The only other way of earning a living from music—and the one
that suited Schubert best—was to write works to order, for

**The Court Theatre (the domed building at the back left of the picture).
Schubert's ambition was to have one of his operas performed here;
but he had no success.**

money. He wrote his first piece of this kind when he was nineteen. An entry in his diary for 17 June 1816 reads:

> Today I composed for money for the first time. Namely, a cantata for the nameday of Professor Wattrot, words by Dräxler. The fee is 100 florins.

This cantata, *Prometheus*, is a large-scale work for two soloists, chorus and orchestra—even for a fast worker like Schubert, at least two weeks' work. The fee was quite generous, enough to live on in comfort for a month. But it was hardly likely that such a large fee, or such interesting words, would come his way every time. More typical is another cantata of the same year, also for soloists, chorus and orchestra. Its fee is not known; but its title suggests that the words were unlikely to offer a composer the highest possible inspiration: "Expressions of Gratitude on the part of the Institute of Teachers' Widows at Vienna to the Founder and Principal of the same."

Schubert wrote dozens of pieces of this kind, all through his life: pieces for birthdays, weddings, funerals; expressions of joy or sadness at the arrival or departure of kings, princes or simply people's friends; song-settings of people's own words, and so on. He usually avoided making them large-scale works with orchestra, and instead produced songs, choruses or short piano pieces. But the work was not regular or predictable, and can only have brought in enough to live on for a very few weeks of each year.

The best guarantee of earning a regular income from commissions—and of keeping the quality and inspiration high—was to write the kind of music publishers wanted to publish. For an Austrian composer, this meant not large-scale orchestral pieces or operas, but smaller pieces, often for domestic or amateur music-making: songs, part-songs, piano solos and duets. Schubert was expert at this, and much of his best, and best-loved, music is of this kind. A list of the works published in 1828 (the year of his death, when he was thirty-one) shows the sort of music publishers wanted—and also that a perfectly satisfactory income could be made by writing it. Thirteen hundred florins was not a fortune, but it was quite enough for one person to live on for a year.

	florins
Songs:	
The Winter Journey (24 songs)	500
3 songs to words by Goethe	75
3 songs to words by Walter Scott	75
18 other songs at 20 florins each	360
Piano music:	
Musical Moments, two books	60
Waltzes	30
2 other works	60
Part songs:	
3 male-voice quartets	90
Chamber music:	
Piano Trio in E flat	about 50
Total	about 1300

Schubert had many friends, some of them well-to-do. Most of them were as easy-going about money as he was himself. Whoever had cash in his pocket paid the bill, and no one kept accounts of loans or debts. Sometimes Schubert's friends paid his rent for a month, invited him to stay, or even gave him money for holidays. Sometimes he himself was the one with money, and he gave a party or took his friends to the theatre. Some writers have

This picture – part drawing, part cartoon – shows a dance in a rich merchant's house in Schubert's time. He went to many dances like this one, and often wrote waltzes and other music for dancing.

thought of him as a scrounger, others as a poverty-stricken genius starving in an attic; but the truth is probably that although he was never very well off, he earned quite enough money to live on, and earned it by writing the songs and chamber music that are still among his best-regarded works.

MUSIC TO LISTEN TO

One of the finest songs written for a special purpose is "The Shepherd on the Rock" (*Der Hirt auf dem Felsen*) for voice, clarinet and piano. The part-songs are rarely performed: two of the best are "Spring Song" (*Frühlingsgesang*) and "Song of the Spirits over the Water" (*Gesang der Geister über den Wassern*). For instrumental music, begin with the three Sonatinas for Violin and Piano (enjoyable to play as well as to hear, and not too difficult). Excerpts from the stage works are sometimes performed: the best to begin with is the incidental music from *Rosamunde*, and *The Twin Brothers* (*Die Zwillingsbrüder*) is worth tracking down.

Chamber music

MUSIC WITH PIANO

For most of the eighteenth century pianos were rare, experimental or luxury instruments, owned mainly by the rich. Ordinary people kept other keyboard instruments at home: spinets, fortepianos, clavichords, small harpsichords. But by Schubert's time piano-makers had found ways of making pianos better and cheaper. Instead of grand pianos, they experimented with smaller, upright or table-shaped models which would fit into the average-sized room. Factories were designed to turn out large numbers of identical models, reliable in quality and not too dear. Pianos soon became standard pieces of furniture, to be found in most middle-class homes.

Publishers were quick to provide music for home use. Hundreds of easy piano solos, duets, and songs with piano were published. For those who wanted larger, harder pieces, publishers provided chamber music: sonatas for violin and piano, trios, quartets and quintets for strings and piano. These works were performed in public as well as by amateur musicians: people liked to go out and hear works they could also play at home. Chamber music was a sociable thing—playing trios or quartets was a splendid way to pass an evening with your friends.

Schubert's chamber music with piano is ideal for this purpose. It is energetic and quite difficult to play, but light-hearted and easy on the ear. He wrote sonatinas, a sonata and a fantasy for violin and piano, several works for piano trio (violin, cello and piano), and one quintet for violin, viola, cello, double bass and piano—almost a roomful of performers.

The quintet is nicknamed the "Trout" Quintet, because the fourth movement is a set of variations on his song "The Trout". It is almost like a miniature piano concerto: the piano part is brilliant and showy, and the strings often play calmer accompanying music. In this example the tune of "The Trout" is played by cello and double bass; the other strings play accompanying chords, and the piano decorates the harmony with showers of fast, light notes:

(not too fast)

For us today, one of the delights of pieces like this is what the composer Schumann called "heavenly length". For thirty or forty minutes the music flows pleasantly on, always varied, always changing, but never too violent or surprising to break our mood. (Schubert himself compared this music to going on a country walk.) Some Viennese critics, however, were used to shorter, more forceful works, and found his pieces rambling and flabby. On 7 February 1828 one newspaper review of a public performance of the *Fantasy* for violin and piano had this to say:

> The *Fantasy* . . . occupied rather too much of the time a Viennese is prepared to devote to pleasures of the mind. The hall emptied gradually, and the writer confesses that he, too, is unable to say anything about the conclusion of this piece of music.

Not all Schubert's chamber music is quite so amiable and easy-going. When he wrote chamber music for strings alone, he was very much aware of the example of Beethoven, whose powerful, tough-sounding quartets he greatly admired. As a boy, he wrote a dozen or so short works for quartet-evenings with his father and brothers. Then, towards the end of his life, he wrote three large-scale quartets which are among his finest and most tightly-organised works. The musical style of the first of them, the Quartet in A minor, is very close to Beethoven's Symphony No 7,

The Vienna woods: one of Schubert's favourite walks. This is a modern photo – but the woods have hardly changed since Schubert's time.

which was first performed in Vienna when Schubert was fifteen, and made a great impression on the public. The Quartet in D minor is often known as "Death and the Maiden", because its beautiful slow movement is a set of variations on Schubert's song of that name.

The most striking of all the chamber works for strings is the Quintet in C, written in 1828 (the last year of Schubert's life, when he was thirty-one). For this work a second cello is added to the normal string quartet. This allows the first cello at times to leave the bass line, and play high up on its plaintive top notes, which helps to give the Quintet an unusually rich and sombre sound. Some of the music is very complex indeed: once again, Schubert had learned from the style of Beethoven's chamber music. Passages like this, for example, must have seemed very difficult, very "modern", to players and audiences of the time:

In 1824, aged twenty-seven, Schubert wrote his longest and largest chamber work, the Octet. This calls for string quartet, double bass, clarinet, bassoon and horn—a large group, suitable for only the grandest living rooms. In fact the work was written for an aristocratic household. It was dedicated to "Count F. von Troyer, chief officer of the household to Archduke Rudolph, Beethoven's patron". Troyer was an amateur clarinettist, and the clarinet player in the Octet is given particularly interesting music to play.

As well as being composed for friends and patrons of Beethoven the Octet pays tribute to him in another way. It takes its basic shape from a chamber work of Beethoven's, the Septet of 1803—a favourite piece with the Viennese public. Schubert adds one instrument (double bass) to Beethoven's seven, but keeps the same pattern of movements, and the same light-hearted, bubbling style. In fact, the style of the Octet is very like that of the Serenades and Divertimentos composers had written for aristocratic patrons in the previous century.

Perhaps because of its aristocratic connections, the Octet was better reviewed than any other chamber work by Schubert. Even so, after its first public performance in 1827, one critic noted its closeness to Beethoven, and also put in the usual complaint about length:

> Herr Schubert's composition is commensurate with the author's acknowledged talent, luminous, agreeable and interesting; only it is possible that too great a claim may be made on the hearer's attention by its long duration. If the themes do not fail to recall familiar ideas by some distant

resemblances, they are nevertheless worked out with individual originality, and Herr Schubert has proved himself, in this species as well, as a gallant and felicitous composer.

Nowadays the Octet is one of Schubert's most familiar and popular pieces, Typical of its carefree, happy style is the last movement, when, after a gloomy, serious introduction, the strings begin a bustle of notes, and a bouncy tune which sets the pace for the whole movement:

MUSIC TO LISTEN TO

Begin with the "Trout" Quintet. If you like that, move on to the Octet, and then to the Piano Trio in B flat. The best of the more serious, Beethoven-inspired pieces to hear first is the String Quintet in C. From that, move on to the three string quartets: the "Death and the Maiden" quartet is perhaps the best to hear first.

Schubert's Vienna

Throughout Schubert's boyhood, Viennese political life was in turmoil. The problem was the French and their leader Napoleon. The Austrians had been at war with France since 1792, three years after the start of the French Revolution. Although they had never suffered crushing defeat, they had never won either. Every year there were threats of new battles or invasions; the whole of Europe was darkened by the grim effects of the war.

For the Viennese, the worst times of all were in 1805 and 1809, when the city was occupied by the French army. Napoleon set up his court in Schönbrunn Palace. Every day he galloped through the streets, surrounded by officers and courtiers. His soldiers paraded and exercised in the city parks; they filled the lodgings and eating houses, and were billeted in private homes. French money, French manners and the French language were everywhere.

Viennese aristocrats found Napoleon terrifying, and his soldiers vulgar and crude. But things were even worse for ordinary people. Many families had lost their breadwinners during the Napoleonic Wars: over a million Austrian soldiers died between 1792 and Napoleon's final defeat at Waterloo in 1814. War conditions in Vienna led to overcrowding, rationing and shortages of every kind. Sometimes the famine was so bad that there was rioting in the streets.

Safe at school, Schubert seems to have been sheltered from most of this upheaval. Neither he nor his family were involved with the army, and riots and rationing were hardly mentioned.

Only once, in a letter to his elder brother of 24 November 1812, when he was fifteen, is there a hint that food shortages might be affecting the meals in school:

> I have long been thinking about my situation, and found that although satisfactory on the whole, it is not beyond improvement here and there. You know from experience that we all like to eat a roll and a few apples sometimes, the more so if after a middling lunch one may not look for a miserable evening meal for eight and a half hours. This wish, which has often become insistent, is now becoming more and more frequent, and I had willy-nilly to make a change. The (pocket-money) I receive from Father goes . . . the very first days, and what am I to do for the rest of the time? . . . How if you were to let me have a few kreuzer a month?

SECRET POLICE

During the Napoleonic Wars, every country in Europe suffered hardship and loss. In 1814, when it was clear that Napoleon's power was certain to be defeated, the princes of Europe decided to settle things so that nothing like it could ever happen again. They gathered in Vienna for an international congress, to sort out the whole future of Europe. Six rulers, with their courtiers, diplomats, advisers and servants took up residence in the city. For nine months, over a hundred thousand foreigners were quartered there, equal to a third of the total population, and far more than any invading army had ever been.

One of the most striking things about the Congress of Vienna was the large number of secret police it brought to the city. Each ruler had his own special agents, and they all went round spying

24

on each other. Men with notebooks lurked everywhere to take down gossip and scandal; letters were steamed open at the post office; daily intelligence reports were passed to each of the rulers.

The Viennese were quite used to spies and secret police. In the 1780s the Emperor Joseph II had set up a large Intelligence Department, and his suspicious successor Francis I (who ruled from 1792 to 1835) enlarged and increased it. The secret police were interested in everything. One of Schubert's friends, Joseph van Spaun, was a keen swimmer, and this nearly got him into trouble, as swimming and acrobatics were frowned on by the authorities because they thought that secret messages could be passed underwater, or while the spectators' eyes were distracted by acrobatic displays.

Of course, not everyone took this sort of thing seriously: as many people laughed at the police as were afraid of them. But even so, you had to be careful. Schubert himself got into trouble in March 1820, when he was twenty-three. One of his friends, Joseph Senn, was suspected of joining a students' union, something not allowed by the authorities. The police called at Senn's lodgings, and found Senn, Schubert and some others there. The young men made fun of them, and were promptly arrested. This extract is from a report made by the Commissioner of Police:

Concerning the stubborn and insulting behaviour of Johann Senn . . . on being arrested as one of the Freshmen Students' Association, on the occasion of the examination and confiscation of his papers carried out by regulation in his lodgings, during which he used the expressions, among others, that he "did not care a hang about the police", and further, that "the Government was too stupid to be able to penetrate into his secrets". It is also said that his friends who were present, Schubert the school-assistant . . . the law-student Streinsberg . . . the undergraduate Zechenter . . . and the son of the wholesale-dealer Bruchmann . . . chimed in against the authorised official in the same tone . . . with insulting and opprobrious language . . . The Chief Constable observes that this report will be taken into consideration during the proceedings against Senn; moreover, those individuals who have conducted themselves rudely towards the High Commissioner of Police . . . will be called and severely reprimanded, and at the same time the Court Secretary Streinsberg as well as the wholesale dealer Bruchmann will be informed of their sons' conduct.

A PLEASANT LIFE

Some people (like the unfortunate Senn, whose career was ruined by that adventure) must have thought troubled politics and police harassment the most important facts of Viennese life. Others, however, like the English traveller Vincent Novello, regarded them as no more than a nuisance, unconnected with the real delights that Vienna had to offer. In his diary for 21 July 1829 Novello wrote:

Of all the troublesome cities to travellers this is surely the worst: pestered at the gates with searching the luggage, fretted with impertinent questions by the police regarding your age, station and fortune; and, to crown all, insulted by a *permit* to remain a stated time in their trumpery city, which if you exceed, you are likely to visit the interior of their well-contrived prisons . . . but to make up for the little provocations

Schubert aged about 25.

upon entering this capital, it must be confessed that the inhabitants are very friendly and hospitable.

Many people regarded Vienna as one of the most beautiful cities in all Europe, and its people as kind, civilised and charming. Middle-class Viennese (like Schubert and his wide circle of friends) often turned away from the harshness of the outside world, and lived a comfortable life of warmth, good food and drink, singing, dancing, and above all the pleasures of friendship.

The Viennese were famous for talking: gossip, scandal and conversation all day and sometimes all night. There were over eighty coffee-shops in the city: places to meet your friends for coffee or hot chocolate, sticky pastries and cakes, dominoes, billiards, the newspapers—and above all, conversation. The city was full of restaurants, bars and dance-halls; and, in an age with no mechanical entertainments like television or the cinema, afternoon- and evening-parties were a favourite way to pass the time.

Another favourite activity, especially in summer, was strolling or riding in the city. A French visitor described the scene like this:

> Country walks, music and dancing in the fresh air, always accompanied by good fare, are habitual among all classes of the population. At the end of the day, if time allows, the suburban artisan takes off his working clothes and puts on a neat suit; with his wife and children he goes to eat fried chicken in one of the innumerable small inns scattered over the rich countryside through which the Danube flows ... (There are) superior restaurants for the lower middle class and well-to-do artisans; in the public gardens which form a green belt round the town, the avenues are copiously supplied

with refreshments and solid viands. In the centre of the gardens a huge space is always set aside for dancing, and numerous bands play waltzes and operatic selections.

To some people this life did seem a little too comfortable, too self-satisfied. They gave it a sarcastic name: the Biedermeier style. (Herr Biedermeier was a character invented in a humorous magazine: he was a good-natured, simple soul who wanted a pleasant life uncomplicated by nasty things like having to think for himself.) Not all Viennese lived like that, of course, but the style was common during Schubert's lifetime, and for another thirty or forty years as well.

This cartoon shows an outdoor concert in the park called the Prater. Eating, drinking, joking, talking to a pedlar (on the left): no one is listening to the musicians.

Schubert wrote hundreds of short dances, often not more than sixteen bars long. Many are in the popular Viennese styles of the *ländler* (a slow, easy-going country dance in three-time), or the waltz. The collections for piano solo are easy to play and enjoyable: look especially for the ones called *Valses Nobles* and *Valses Sentimentales*. The piano duet music contains many groups of dances and marches. The three *Military Marches* are the best known, but just as good are the *Ländler* and the two sets of *Polonaises*. A larger work, *Divertissement à l'Hongroise*, makes something more important out of short dance forms. Dance ideas are

Music in a Viennese tavern. This kind of entertainment filled many evenings for Schubert and his friends.

worked into many large-scale works: the last movement of the String Quintet and the third and fourth movements of the String Quartet in A minor are good examples. Many minuets or scherzos include sections in *ländler*-style: those in the Quartet in D minor and Symphony No 9 are among the finest.

Symphonies

SCHUBERT AND THE ORCHESTRA

In the eighteenth century there were no public orchestras like those of today. Where orchestras existed at all, they were private: they belonged to opera houses and perfomed only there, or were employed as court musicians by rich aristocrats, and played only for their patrons and their guests. Towards the end of the century some composers—Mozart, for example—developed the idea of giving public concerts for money. But instead of using existing orchestras, as composers would today, they had to assemble and train an orchestra especially for each concert.

Once concert-going caught on, and musicians found that they could make a regular living playing in public, more and more orchestras were founded. In most cities and big towns, music-lovers clubbed together to form Concert Societies and Philharmonic Societies—and these societies created their own orchestras to give public concerts of interesting new music as well as works of the past.

Vienna had several such societies. The two most famous, each with its own choir and orchestra, were the Vienna Philharmonic

Society and the *Gesellschaft der Musikfreunde* (Society of the Friends of Music). Most of their concerts were built round music of the past, including many works by Haydn and Mozart; but they also encouraged living composers, particularly Beethoven. As well as

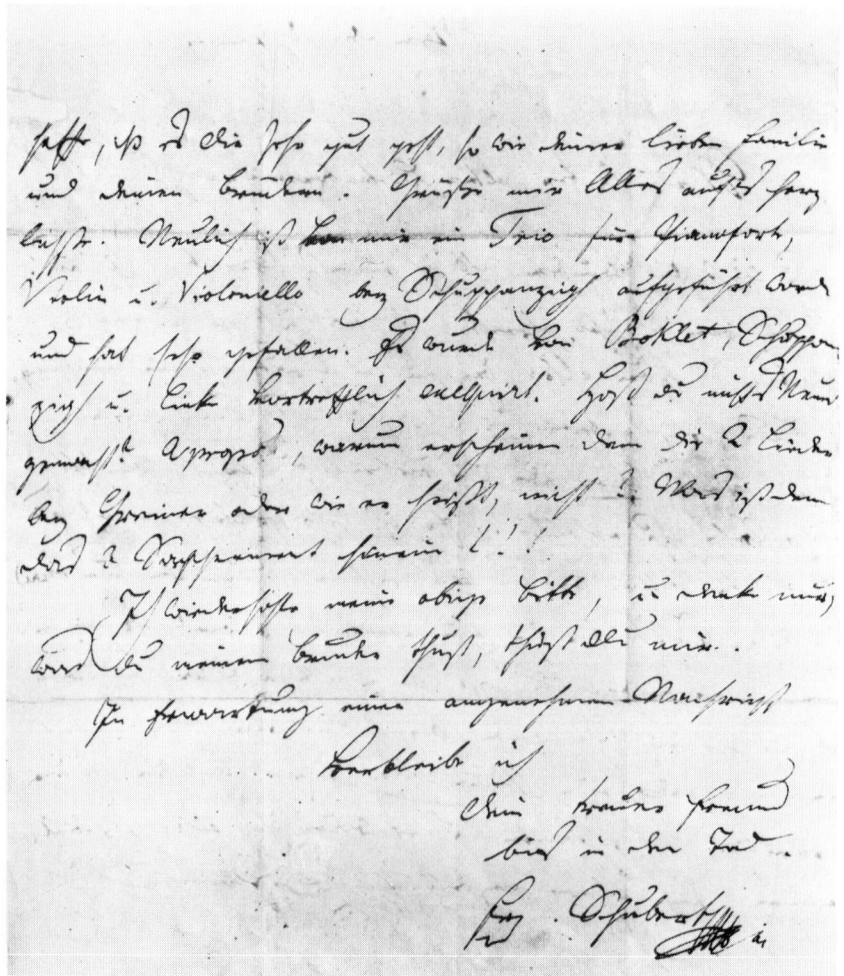

Schubert's handwriting – a letter of 1828.

these large, high-quality orchestras, there were several smaller ones. The school orchestra of Schubert's Imperial Seminary gave occasional public concerts, and he was also involved, as a young man, with a small "rehearsal orchestra" which regularly met to play through new works by young composers.

Schubert's first three symphonies were probably written for the school orchestra. They are not "great music", towering masterpieces like the symphonies of Beethoven; but they are easy-going and charming, a pleasure to play and to listen to. The players are never over-taxed: he must have known all the performers personally, and heard them practising, and he was careful to give them music he knew they could play. The bassoon and cello parts, for example, are clearly written for less expert performers than the violins or the other woodwind players. The brass parts are very easy, but skilfully placed to make the best effect with the fewest notes.

These works, however, are not simply training pieces for school musicians. Schubert was learning his own craft of composing as well. The symphonies are modelled on the style of the best works of the time, and Schubert obviously learned a lot from the symphonies of Mozart in particular. The music is light-weight, but expert.

The next three symphonies, written for the "rehearsal orchestra" of Schubert's friends, are a great advance on the school symphonies. In the first place, they were written for more experienced players. Many of them were professional musicians who came to play in the orchestra because they were interested in new

33

music. They had experience of other orchestras and other music, and knew how to get the best possible effect out of playing together. In the second place, Schubert was much more certain of himself as a composer. At the time of the early symphonies, he had written only a few dozen works. But by the time of Symphony No 4 (1816, when he was nineteen), he had composed several hundred songs, piano and chamber works, and had heard a good deal of his music performed. The influences of Mozart, Haydn and Beethoven are still there in the music, but now he is not just imitating them, but adapting and changing their style to suit his own ideas.

Nowadays the favourite of these works is Symphony No 5 in B flat. Many people find it one of the happiest and most sparkling of all Schubert's compositions. It is also one of the most skilfully written. A good example is the passage opposite, from the slow movement. Over a murmuring accompaniment, the violins and woodwind play short phrases which answer each other as if in a conversation. Then, towards the end of the example, the key changes from major to minor, and the same answering phrases change instruments: the violins play the woodwind phrase, and vice versa. The effect is simple, but full of craftsmanship—what is sometimes called "the simplicity of genius".

LATER SYMPHONIES

After Symphony No 6 in C, Schubert's ambitions for his symphonies seem to have changed. He was particularly anxious to write what he called a "Grand Symphony", a large work like the symphonies of Beethoven. Even more important, he was anxious that once it was written, it should be performed by a really professional orchestra.

But these ambitions were not easy to fulfil. He made several attempts at writing "Grand Symphonies". In 1821 (when he was twenty-four) he wrote a Symphony in E, complete from first bar to last, but not fully arranged for orchestra. The draft is a hundred and sixty-seven pages long, and he may have wanted to be sure of a performance before starting the immense job of writing out an orchestral score. The performance never came, and the work still remains in draft. (This symphony is counted as Number 7 in the complete list.)

A year later, in 1822, he wrote parts of another symphony, No 8 in B minor. Two movements were completed and scored for orchestra, and sketches made for at least one other movement. He began to look round for ways of getting the symphony performed. His first idea seems to have been to join the Vienna Philharmonic Society as a viola-player, and persuade them to give the first performance. But he was unsuccessful: the rules of the Society, it is said, allowed only amateur musicians to be elected, not professionals. Next, on 20 September 1823, he wrote to the Music Society at Graz:

> Gentlemen of the Musical Society,
>
> I am very greatly obliged by the diploma of honorary membership you so kindly sent me, and which, owing to my prolonged absence from Vienna, I received only a few days ago. May it be the reward of my devotion to the art of music to become wholly worthy of such a distinction one day. In order to give musical expression to my sincere gratitude as well, I shall take the liberty before long of presenting your honourable society with one of my symphonies in full score.
>
> With the highest regards, I remain your honourable society's most grateful, devoted and obedient servant,
> Franz Schubert.

No one really knows whether the symphony he meant was actually No 8 or another one. The Society at Graz never performed a Schubert symphony, and Symphony No 8 remained unperformed for another forty years. Nowadays it is Schubert's most famous and most often performed work. Although some people have published completed versions, the one usually played consists of the first two movements only—they seem so satisfying that it is hard, now, to imagine what the "Unfinished" Symphony would be like if Schubert *had* finished it.

In 1825, aged twenty-seven, Schubert went for a summer

Schubert - a famous portrait by one of his friends.

holiday in the Alps at Gastein. Here, according to his friends, he wrote a "Grand Symphony in C", and it was one of his own favourites among his works. What happened to it is a mystery. Some people think it is the Symphony No 9 in C (nicknamed "The Great C major" to distinguish it from Symphony No 6, "The Little C major"). Whether this is the "Gastein" Symphony or not, it first appeared three years later in Vienna in 1828, and is the only complete "Grand Symphony" of Schubert's that survives today. This is the work turned down by the players of the Vienna Philharmonic Society, who found it too long and difficult to rehearse in time. Like the "Unfinished", it was not performed in Schubert's own lifetime, but has since become one of his most popular works.

Both the "Unfinished" and the "Great C Major" are on an entirely different scale from Schubert's earlier symphonies. Their movements are nearly twice as long, and the orchestra is larger, with added horns and trombones. The music itself is large and impressive, in a grand manner unlike any of his other works. The photograph on page 39 shows a typical page from the "Unfinished". The whole orchestra is playing loud, wide-spaced chords in a solemn, throbbing style. The *fz* marks (meaning "attack with force"), the loud harmony on the brass instruments (in the middle of the page), and the hammering of the drums (*timpani*) make a larger, fuller effect than in any of his music written up to that time.

The best of the early symphonies to listen to is Symphony No 3 in D. After this, move on to Symphony No 5 in B flat, and then

to the last two, the "Unfinished" Symphony No 8 in B minor and
the "Great C Major" Symphony, No 9.

"Unfinished Symphony", first movement.

Piano music

Like many composers, Schubert was an excellent pianist. Most of his song accompaniments—some requiring the greatest skill—were written in the first place for himself to play, and he was always ready to play piano solos for his friends. Their letters and diaries are full of comments like this one from Hartmann's diary for 8 December 1826:

> At 8.30 I went to Spaun's, where the two brothers and Fritz were at first. Then came Schubert, and played a magnificent but melancholy piece of his own composition.

Schubert's piano, in a corner of his lodgings. It is littered with music, letters and books of poems.

Schubert's piano music (whether solo, for one performer, or duet, for two) can be divided into two kinds. First, there are "lighter" works: rondos, polonaises, marches, "musical moments", impromptus and dances. Publishers were clamouring for this kind of music, to satisfy the growing number of amateur pianists all over Europe. Second come much larger, "grander" pieces: eleven solo sonatas; a "Grand Fantasy" for solo piano, and another for piano duet; a sonata and a "Grand Duo" for piano duet.

These large-scale piano works are among Schubert's most serious compositions. In several of them he was inspired by the example of Beethoven's piano sonatas, and set out to produce big, "heroic" music of the same kind. Others are like the "Unfinished" or "Great C Major" symphonies in style and sound—so much so that some people think they may be piano arrangements of "lost" orchestral works like the "Gastein" symphony of 1825.

PIANO SOLO

Schubert's easiest, most light-hearted piano music comes in collections of dances, probably written actually *for* dancing. The music has attractive tunes, and its rhythms are easy to follow. This example comes from a collection called "Homage to the Pretty Girls of Vienna", published in 1826:

Other single pieces (meant for listening, not dancing) include several of Schubert's best-known compositions, favourites almost since the day they were written. He understood exactly the sort of music to provide: not hair-raisingly difficult but still able to stretch the fingers; not hard to listen to, but still more than just "light music". The best of these works are the two collections of *Impromptus* (Op 90 and Op 142), and the *Moments Musicaux* (Musical Moments, Op 94).

The finest of his solo piano music comes in large-scale, "grand" works like the *Wanderer Fantasia* and the piano sonatas. Like Beethoven, Schubert seems to have enjoyed improvising at the piano: that is, making the music up as he went along, experimenting, not hindered by the need to write anything down. Very often these improvisations gave him ideas which he later worked into written compositions. His piano sonatas often contain unusual, experimental ideas, as if they were a kind of musical diary into which he put his most personal thoughts. This quality of imagination (or "fantasy", as it was called) impressed critics and friends alike. Writing (1 March 1826) of the Piano Sonata in A minor, Op 42, one critic said:

> Many musical pieces nowadays bear the name of Fantasy, though fantasy has had very little share in them, if any at all . . . Here, on the contrary, a composition for once bears the name of Sonata, though it was fantasy, quite evidently, which had the largest and most decisive share in it . . . Although it preserves a praiseworthy unity, it moves freely and originally within its confines, and sometimes so boldly and curiously, that it might not unjustly have been called a Fantasy. In that respect it can probably be compared only with the greatest and freest of Beethoven's sonatas.

Some months before, Schubert had played the same sonata to his friends. On 25 July 1825 he described their reaction in a letter to his father—and also gave some idea of the sort of piano-playing he admired, and the kind he tried to avoid:

What pleased especially were the variations in my new sonata for two hands, which I performed alone and not without merit, since several people assured me that the keys became singing voices under my hands. Which, if true, pleases me greatly, since I cannot endure the accursed chopping in which even distinguished pianoforte players indulge, and which delights neither the ear nor the mind.

PIANO DUETS

To many musicians of Schubert's time, piano duets were not something to take very seriously. If you went to visit friends, the chances were high that your host's daughters would sit down at the piano and tinkle their way through a selection of charming, pretty pieces, while everyone clucked and murmured with admiration. For middle-class girls, playing piano duets was as much part of growing up as embroidery or painting with water-colours. It was genteel and lady-like, a sign of good education, breeding and taste.

Some of Schubert's duet music consists of short marches, waltzes and variations, just right for this kind of drawing-room entertainment. But most of it would have filled the average drawing-room listener with surprise—and really exercised any drawing-room pianists who tried to learn it. The two players have to be excellent musicians, who understand each other's style and work to produce a seamless, easy flow of music, as if one single mind is in control. Many of the works are too long and serious to be used for passing the time.

Two of Schubert's greatest works are for piano duet: *Fantasia in F minor* and *Grand Duo in C*. This is not drawing-room music. It calls for the finest of pianos, the largest of halls, the most attentive of audiences. It is filled with the same powerful imagination, the

Steyr, a village in the Austrian countryside. Schubert's friends often took him for summer holidays in Alpine resorts like this.

same "fantasy", as the critic above found in the A minor solo sonata. A passage like this, for example, from the *Grand Duo*, would hardly be out of place in the largest of symphonies:

The lay-out of piano duets is particularly well suited to the sound of Schubert's music. He wrote a rich, full kind of harmony, using full chords spread over the whole range of notes from high to low. In a piano duet, the lower player's right hand plays round about the middle of the keyboard, where the sound is particularly rich and sonorous. In two-handed music this part of the keyboard often has to be ignored, as the hands are playing lower down or higher up. But in four-handed music it is one of the main ingredients of the sound, and adds the same kind of richness as brass instruments often do in Schubert's orchestral music. In the upper part, the player often plays the same melody with both hands; this, too, produces a bright, full sound difficult for a single player to manage on his own. Passages like this, for example, from the

Rondo in A, sound full and sonorous in a way no single player
could ever achieve:

There is so much Schubert piano music, all of it enjoyable, that
the best advice is probably to explore it for yourself. Where you
can, play it as well as listening: it lies well under the fingers, and
is particularly satisfying to browse through. For solo music, begin
with the *Impromptus* Op 90 and Op 142, and the *Moments Musicaux*
Op 94. Then move on to the sonatas. The Sonata in A Op 120 is a
good one to begin with, followed by the Sonata in G Op 78 and
the Sonata in B flat (1828). If you like those, you should enjoy any
of the others, or the *Wanderer Fantasia*, just as much.

For duet music, begin with the easy dances, then move on to
Andante in A, Divertissement à l'Hongroise and the *Sonata in B flat*.
Then listen to perhaps the best pieces of all: *Fantasia in F minor*
and *Grand Duo in C*.

46

Schubert's friends

In a newspaper interview published a few months after Schubert's death, one of his friends wrote:

> Between nine o'clock in the morning and two o'clock in the afternoon, Schubert daily and without exception devoted himself to composition or to his studies. But the afternoon and evening were given up to his family and friends. No feast, no repast, no entertainment gave him pleasure if it was not seasoned by friendly intercourse. To the beauties of nature he was most receptive, and on fine summer days he almost daily made longish excursions into the beautiful environs of Vienna in the afternoons and evenings. He had a particularly great predilection in this respect for the glorious regions of Upper Austria and Salzburg, which for several years he visited with Vogl in the summer months.

Looking back nowadays, it is easy to imagine that everyone who knew Schubert must have realised he was a genius, and treated him with suitable awe and respect. But they never did. They enjoyed his singing and playing, and thought highly of some of his compositions. But, as the quotation above suggests, he was chiefly valued as a friend, someone who liked good food and drink, conversation and long walks in the country. His nickname was *Schwammerl* ("Stocky"), and it is clear from his friends' writings that he was always right at the heart of whatever fun was going on. New Year's Eve 1824, when he was twenty-seven, is typical:

Our New Year's Eve festivity went off happily. We gathered at Mohn's. Bruchmann and Doblhoff returned on the stroke of twelve from the city, where they had expected and sought Schubert. You, Senn and Kupelweiser, Bruchmann and everybody's sweethearts all had their health drunk. Soon afterwards, Schubert and Dr Bernhardt announced themselves by a small target-shooting match. Schubert hit, and the shattered window pane set everyone astir . . . I got home at four thirty a.m. It was all a bit crude and common, but better than we might have expected.

Reading that, we may be reminded of some of the characters of Dickens, particularly Mr Pickwick and his friends. They are ordinary, middle-class people, not particularly rich or important; their lives are comfortable and contented, free from struggles and upheavals. Herr Biedermeier (page 29) would have approved of them: solid citizens, honest, hard-working, with their hearts in the right place. They had an extra quality, too, which Biedermeier might not have appreciated so highly: imagination.

All but a few of Schubert's friends worked for a living. Some were in the Civil Service, working for the State Lottery, for example, or in the Censor's department. Others were teachers or lawyers. A few had more unusual jobs. One, a doctor, had studied hypnotism and mesmerism (a kind of early psychiatry, fashionable in Vienna at the time); another worked in theatre administration; another ran an art gallery; another, Vogl, was a famous singer, elderly and losing his voice for opera, but still popular with concert-goers (for whom he regularly performed Schubert's songs).

Like Schubert himself, they spent the early part of each day working. Then, several evenings a week, they gathered in coffee-shops, restaurants, or each other's houses, to eat, drink, chat, listen to music, play cards, do conjuring tricks (sometimes juggling or acrobatics), and then move on to the dance-hall, theatre, bar or opera house. These four short passages give a

A cartoon of Schubert and his tall friend Vogl, who gave the first performance of many of his songs (see page 56).

glimpse of what their life was like (the first three evenings took place in a single week):

5 December 1826: I went to the Anchor, where Schober, Schubert and Lachner (a composer from Bavaria) were at first, and only late and unexpectedly Pepi Spaun, with whom we remained until midnight, he telling us splendid stories of his and his brother's youth.

7 December 1826: To the Anchor at nine forty-five; Schober, Pepi Spaun and Schubert there. Home at eleven thirty.

8 December 1826: At eight thirty I went to Spaun's, where the two brothers and Fritz were at first. Then came Schubert and played a magnificent but melancholy piece of his own composition. At last Schwind, Bauernfeld, Enderes and Schober came too. Schubert and Schwind then sang the most lovely Schubert songs. In the end we supped splendidly. All were very lively and wide awake. At last everybody began to smoke. Spax, naturally enough, very often dozed off. At twelve forty-five we parted. We saw Schober home.

14 January 1827: When we have breakfasted (at Spaun's), Gahy plays some very fine German dances of Schubert's. Enderes juggles beautifully with sticks, rods and the like; I try to emulate him and let a stick on which a steel hammer was balanced drop heavily on his forehead, which gives me a terrible fright. I could no longer listen to the dances at all, but stayed with him all the time while he bathed the swelling and thus fortunately kept it down.

For most of the friends, these gatherings were clearly a way of relaxing and enjoying themselves. But for Schubert himself, they were sometimes more than that. Often when he sat down to play or sing, it was entirely for fun: people chatted, smoked (and even juggled) while the music was going on. But at other times his performance was much more serious. Music was the main event of the evening, and his friends gathered especially to listen to it. He liked to play his latest works to a group who knew and liked his music, and obviously valued their comments and reactions. (These were not always favourable: they found the "Winter Journey" song cycle, for example, lugubrious and hard to follow.)

A dance in the Prater.

A Schubertiad. Vogl sings; Schubert accompanies; the friends listen
in delight.

Gatherings of this kind often attracted a larger group than just the close circle of friends. For some of them, as many as forty or fifty people might be invited. A special name was given them: the friends were called "Schubertians", and the evenings themselves "Schubertiads". As this description of a Schubertiad on 12 January 1827 shows, the mood could change in a moment, from serious listening to boisterous horseplay and fun:

12 January 1827: To Spaun's where there is a Schubertiad. The dear Witteczek couple and his mother-in-law are there already: tall Huber too. Then, one by one, came Gahy, Schober, Schubert, Enderes, Walcher (who however had to leave before the music began), Moritz Pflügel (who has been in Paris), Lachner, a certain Preder, Perfetter; finally Vogl and his wife. Bauernfeld, Schwind, Gross. We had a splendid piano sonata for four hands, glorious variations and many magnificent songs, among them a brand-new one (sung by Richard Coeur de Lion in *Ivanhoe*) and old ones including "Night and Dreams" and "The Erlking". A specially beautiful one, "In the Sunset" (to words by Lappe), was sung twice by Vogl, who happened to be in an exceptionally good mood. Then we had a delicious repast and several toasts were drunk. Suddenly Spaun arrived, and said we must drink to Brother-hood, which much surprised and delighted me. Then we had a tossing in a blanket (Enderes and Huber, the latter behaving very clumsily) and made the well-known beautiful star with four pairs. At last we took our leave of our kind hosts and went helter-skelter to Bogner's, where we smoked a few pipes, and in the street, Schwind, running and flapping his cloak, gave a striking illusion of flying.

The music played at a Schubertiad was generally for piano (solo or duet), or songs. Occasionally chamber music was performed (for example the Piano Trio in E flat, or the Arpeggione Sonata). You could listen to the exact programme of the Schubertiad mentioned in this chapter: it included the *Andantino Varié* and *Grand Duo in C* (both for piano duet), and the songs "Night and Dreams" (*Nacht und Träume*), "The Erlking" (*Der Erlkönig*) and "In the Sunset" (*Im Abendrot*).

Setting off for a ride in the country. This painting shows a group of Schubert's friends, in a hired carriage. Schubert stands on the left of the picture.

Songs

On 30 January 1821 (the day before Schubert's twenty-fourth birthday) a Dresden newspaper published this review:

> The young composer Schubert has set to music several songs by the best poets ... which testify to the profoundest studies, combined with genius worthy of admiration, and attract the eyes of the cultivated musical world. He knows how to paint in sound, and the songs "The Trout", "Gretchen at the Spinning Wheel" ... and "The Combat" ... surpass in characteristic truth all that may be found in the domain of song.

Many people throughout the world would still agree with those comments. Schubert is regarded as one of the finest song-writers there has ever been. Concerts are frequently given consisting of nothing but his songs, and there are singers who make their whole career singing them. The kind of songs he wrote are normally known by their German name, *lieder*: this suggests a larger, deeper kind of music than is normally meant by the English word "song".

In his own lifetime, Schubert's songs were his most often performed and published works. They were eagerly awaited—and usually very well received, as these reviews show:

> *Dresden Abendzeitung*, 26 April 1821: What pleased above all was "The Erlking", which Vogl performed with his accustomed mastery, and which had to be repeated. This splendid composition cannot fail to seize the hearer; it has now appeared in print ... and I am convinced that I shall earn the gratitude

Schubert playing the accompaniment to one of his songs.

of any reader who wishes to procure this masterpiece for having drawn his attention to it.

Vienna Theaterzeitung, 22 May 1821: Newly appeared: "Shepherd's Complaint", "The Wild Rose", "Huntsman's Evening Song" and "Stillness of the Sea", four poems by Goethe, set to music by Franz Schubert. Each of these songs has its own character, according to the poet's intention; delightful melodies and a noble simplicity, alternating with original force and elevation, unite them into a glorious wreath of song, which joins worthily on to the earlier excellent achievements of this talented composer.

Vienna Zeitschrift für Kunst, 23 March 1822: Schubert's songs raise themselves by ever undeniable excellences to the rank of masterpieces of genius, calculated to restore the present debased taste; for never has the true force of genius failed in its effect on heart and mind.

Once published, Schubert's songs were sung all over Europe—they travelled far further than he ever did himself. Strange things happened to some of them, too. His first published song, "The Erlking" (which is about a father trying to save his sick child from being snatched by Death), was arranged and rearranged by publishers. Even during Schubert's lifetime it appeared as a piano solo, a vocal quartet, a song with guitar, a solo for the organ in a musical clock, a set of waltzes, and finally, in the year after his death, a suite of galops for the dance-hall. This fate tells us something about what the last critic called "the present debased taste", but it also shows how popular a particular song could be. As well as in these arranged versions, "The Erlking" was also performed "properly" hundreds of times during Schubert's life, and, with others of his songs, became a popular item at concerts and evening parties all over Europe.

THE STYLE OF SCHUBERT'S SONGS

In most songs before Schubert, the most important thing is the melody. Nothing else matters as much. The accompaniment is there partly to help the singer, and partly to surround the melody and show it at its best—much as a beautiful frame shows off a picture. If the picture matters more than the frame, the frame can be changed; so, in many of these songs, the accompaniment can be arranged for other instruments without seriously affecting the song as a whole.

In Schubert, things are completely different. The piano part has as much effect on the mood and feeling of the song as the voice does. Often it picks up a basic idea in the words, and reminds us of it even when the voice is singing of something else. A good example comes in "The Trout": throughout the song, the piano keeps playing a rippling, leaping phrase that suggests not just the movement of a trout in water, but also its energy, elegance and beauty:

In more complex songs, the accompaniment does more than show us events or movement. Schubert uses it to suggest a mood, an emotion, the feeling at the heart of the song. A good example comes in the song-cycle (or group of songs) "The Maid of the Mill". There are two main "characters" in these songs: the young man who does the singing, and the running brook he sings to, which seems to him to answer and reflect his words. In several of the songs, the piano often has a rippling, bubbling accompaniment, representing the brook. But the emotion of the brook's music can change, to reflect the emotions of the young man walking beside it. In the first song, the ripple is placid and happy: it is a beautiful day and the young man is in love:

By the fifteenth song, we know that the young man's love has turned to despair, and that he feels he is rushing headlong towards disaster. Now the rippling of the brook, too, sounds headlong and threatening:

60

In another song, "The Ghost", piano and voice are even more equal partners. Without the piano the voice-part would be tuneless and meaningless; without the voice the piano part would be a series of strange, unconnected chords. Together they produce an eerie effect that exactly suits the terror and despair in the words. The song is about a lover who returns to his lost beloved's house, and finds a ghost outside wringing its hands—and the ghost is himself. In this example, the start of the song, the words give no clue about menace or eeriness, but the bare piano accompaniment tells us clearly about the lover's feelings of emptiness and despair:

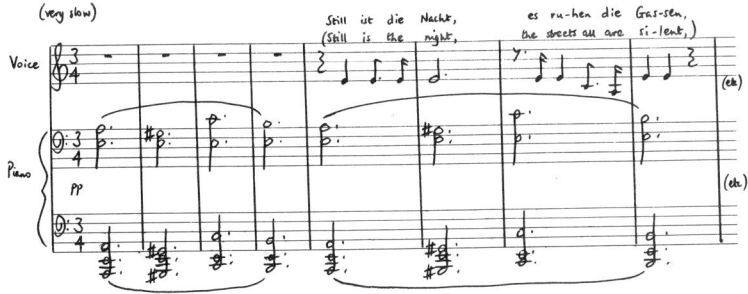

To go so deeply into feelings and emotions, in such a few notes, is a rare gift. Schubert seems to have been able to "fix" the mood of a song almost instantly. Many of his songs were written in the time it took to put the notes on paper—and he seldom made many alterations once the ink was dry. To his friends it was almost miraculous, like a lightning-flash of inspiration.

Part of the secret was certainly his eye for the right words. He seems to have known at once if a poem was right for music, and exactly what music would suit it best. Sometimes he chose poems by great writers: Shakespeare, Goethe and Heine, for example. At other times he set verses by second- or third-rate poets, nowadays

This picture, from the first cover of "The Erlking", shows the romantic view some people of Schubert's time had of the story.

largely forgotten. He used verses of his own, by his friends, and by many of the German and Austrian poets of the day. Sometimes people sent him books of verse, hoping that he would choose something from them; sometimes his friends suggested poems to him, or he found them in newspapers and magazines. Anthologies have been made just of the words of his songs—and they contain the work of over a hundred poets, a fair selection of all the European verse known at the time.

Usually it was enough for Schubert to set a single poem at a time. Some of his songs are short, but many are large-scale compositions lasting ten minutes or more. Twice he wrote something larger still, and published what are now called "song cycles": sets of songs by the same poet on the same theme, to be sung always in the same order, and telling a single story. The first song-cycle, "The Maid of the Mill", contains twenty songs; the second, "Winter Journey", twenty-four. The length of the cycles —over forty minutes—and the ordering of the songs, allows him to show deeper, changing emotion than was possible in a single song. The cycles are rather like symphonies for voice and piano: each section tells you more about the others, and it's not until the end that the whole depth of meaning is clear.

MUSIC TO LISTEN TO

The sheer quantity of Schubert's songs (over six hundred) makes it difficult to make recommendations. *Lieder* recitals, and records of *lieder*, group the individual songs in different ways, according to each singer's taste: but in any grouping there should be plenty for all listeners to enjoy. It's a good idea to find an English translation of the words before you hear the songs.

Perhaps the best way to begin is to listen to collections of separate songs: serious ones like "Ganymede" (*Ganymed*), "The Wanderer" (*Der Wanderer*), "Death and the Maiden" (*Tod und das Mädchen*) and "To Music" (*An die Musik*), or lighter ones like "The Trout" (*Die Forelle*), "The Wild Rose" (*Heidenröslein*) or "Serenade" (*Ständchen*). From them, move on to "Swansong" (*Schwanengesang*), a group of magnificent, unconnected songs composed at the very end of his life, and usually sung and recorded together. After that, try the song-cycles: first "The Maid of the Mill" (*Die Schöne Müllerin*), then "Winter Journey" (*Winterreise*).

Schubert's musical handwriting: the manuscript of his song *Nacht-gesang* **("Nightsong"), written in 1815.**

How Schubert composed

Schubert's composing life, compared to that of many composers, was short: sixteen years, from about 1812, when he was fifteen, to his death in 1828. In that time he wrote an incredible amount of music: symphonies, choral works, operas, chamber music, piano works, cantatas, overtures, dances and over six hundred songs. Writing the year after his death, a friend commented:

> Schubert's rapidity in composition was extraordinary. Whoever . . . gave him a poem to set could be sure that, if the musician liked it, a well-finished composition would be ready the next day. Thus originated the glorious song "The Wanderer" . . .; thus was the reading and setting of Goethe's "The Erlking" the work of an afternoon.

Another friend describes an occasion when, in the middle of a conversation, Schubert seems suddenly to have had a flash of inspiration, an idea which couldn't wait to be put down on paper:

> We do not lack visitors, for we have several each day: Angerer and Jenger come more often than usual, and Schubert too has given us the pleasure once already. He was most amiable and talkative, but escaped suddenly, before anyone had an inkling.

Sudden, unpredictable behaviour like that suited the nineteenth century view of a composer: a genius, not like ordinary people, and likely to be struck with inspiration at any moment. But however the original ideas came, Schubert's actual working

65

habits were more like those of a craftsman than an erratic genius. He worked regular hours, from nine until two every day—and he was quite short with people who interrupted, as another friend reported:

> He has now long been at work on an octet, with the greatest zeal. If you go to see him during the day, he says, "Hullo, how are you? Good!" and goes on writing, whereupon you depart.

Schubert seems to have done much of the hard work of composing in his head, before he set anything down on paper. He probably worked out some of his ideas at the piano; but he might just as easily sit doing nothing, while he thought a piece through in his mind. Once he started writing the notes down, he worked quickly, with few alterations. Particularly in shorter pieces, his manuscripts are very neat, and there are often no changes at all. Once they were written, he put them aside for later performance, or gathered them up to send to a publisher.

If he was writing a long work, like a sonata or symphony, his method seems to have been to get as much on paper as possible. Then, if there was a chance of having it performed, he would go back to it and finish it. But this could be several weeks' or months' work, and sometimes his interest in a long work left him in the middle, and he moved on to something else. Later on he might use the unfinished portions as the basis of another piece; but sometimes he simply ignored them, and left them in a drawer, unfinished forever. Where works *were* completed or revised, the manuscripts are full of alterations and improvements—what one writer called "inspired afterthoughts".

Schubert at work - a painting made at the end of his life.

Schubert was what later came to be called a "romantic" composer. That is, he believed that music, as well as simply existing in its own right, could express thoughts and emotions, and that it had power to touch people's hearts as well as entertaining their minds. In this review of "The Erlking", from a Vienna paper of 23 March 1822, the critic follows up this idea. He tells his readers a great deal about the emotional force of the music, and the feelings he thinks the notes express:

> With profoundly moving truth the melodic expression characterises the inner meaning of the action, the changing emotions of the father, the child and the erlking; while its outward aspects, such as the galloping horse and the inter-mittent howling of the gale, are outlined by the most appropriate figures of accompaniment. Such a treatment was the only possible one in this case, since the uniform romance-like tone of the poem demanded a similarly uniform tone in the musical representation.

In short songs and single piano pieces, a composer can let the emotion guide his musical form, the shape of his piece. Often only one or two ideas are expressed in the music, and it is simple and straightforward to listen to, without needing complicated organ-isation. But in longer works—sonatas, symphonies and long pieces of chamber music—there has to be more control. Feeling and emotion are there, but the hearer's mind also needs recog-nisable musical shapes to follow, or there is a danger of the music sounding rambling or even chaotic.

In the century before Schubert, composers had gradually

developed precise ways of organising long pieces of instrumental music. They are like patterns, basic skeletons which work in the same way for every composer. The listener knows the sort of thing to expect, and his enjoyment comes partly when the composer moves from one expected item to the next, and partly from the new ways he finds of presenting the usual forms. In this controlled, disciplined style (usually called "classical"), most symphonies or sonatas, whoever they are by, have the same number of movements, in the same basic order, and each with its well-known, particular form.

The finest music Schubert knew was in this kind of "classical" style. After his death a friend wrote:

> With the classical works of the great masters Schubert was intimately acquainted, and he felt for them—for Handel, Gluck, Mozart, Haydn and Beethoven—the most enthusiastic reverence.

Because of that reverence, it was natural that when he came to write large-scale pieces of his own, he should at first want to produce something along the same lines as the composers he admired. His early piano sonatas follow Beethoven, his early string quartets Haydn, his early masses and symphonies Mozart. That is, although the music is distinctively Schubert's, it uses "classical" forms and patterns not in an individual way, but in the same way as the older composers he most admired.

As he became more experienced, however, he began to use the classical style in a distinctive, personal way, quite unlike any composers before him. The form of his music, its harmony and its organisation, still followed the basic pattern, but each was

69

modified and adapted until the whole effect was really completely new. Most classical composers, for example, built their movements from short "cells" of a very few notes, which could be developed and modified as the music proceeded. Schubert, instead of "cells", writes melodies up to ten times as long, which cannot be chopped up and developed in the same way. His movements become longer, and the music advances not by constantly developing the same basic note-patterns, but by contrasting several larger, almost unchanging sections one against another.

This also makes it sound more "emotional", more "romantic". A four- or five-note cell is too short to mean much on its own, and takes its meaning from its surroundings and what happens to it. But a melody has time to create a mood of its own, and is less affected by changes in the surrounding music. For many listeners this "mood-painting" was one of the main attractions of Schubert's large-scale music. Even those who found it hard at first were willing to keep trying—like this critic, writing on 27 March 1824 of the String Quartet in A minor:

> New quartet by Schubert. This composition must be heard several times before it can be adequately judged.

MUSIC TO LISTEN TO

Often, when you hear a single song or short piano piece, it will suggest a single emotion only. It is worth comparing your own reaction (to songs like "The Wanderer", "Death and the Maiden" and "The Erlking", or piano pieces like the *Moments Musicaux* Op 94) with someone else's (like that of the critic of "The Erlking" quoted on pages 56–58).

In large-scale works, the difference betwen Schubert's "classical" and "romantic" style can often be heard if you listen to an early work and then a later work of the same kind. The early Mass in F (1814), for example, is straightforward and suitable for church use; but the Mass in A flat (1822) is far longer, more individual, better suited to a concert-hall than a church service. In the same way, the later string quartets (like the Quartet in A minor) are based on the same classical forms as the early ones (like the Quartet in D of 1813), but they are far longer, larger in scale and deeper in thought. The same comparison can be made with other works too, by taking early sonatas or symphonies (Sonata in A flat (1817); Symphony No 4 in C minor) and comparing them with later ones (Sonata in C minor (1828); Symphony No 9 in C).

Schubert remembered

From the diary of his friend BAUERNFELD, *20 November 1828*

Yesterday afternoon Schubert died. On Monday I still spoke with him. On Tuesday he was delirious, on Wednesday dead. To the last he talked to me of our opera. It all seems like a dream to me. The most honest soul and the most faithful friend! I wish I lay there in his place. For he leaves the world with fame!

Memoir by a doctor friend of Schubert, published in 1858

The figure short, but sturdy, with well-developed, solid bones and firm muscles; not angular, but rather rounded . . . hands and feet small; his walk lively and vigorous. The fairly large, round and powerful skull was surrounded by brown, abundantly flowing locks . . . the mild eyes, light brown if I am not mistaken, which could flash when he was excited, were strongly over-shadowed by fairly prominent and bushy eyebrows, and thus seemed smaller than they really were, especially as he often narrowed them, as short-sighted people will. The nose was of a medium size, blunt and tilted up a little, and joined by a gentle inward sweep to his full, abundant, firmly set lips, which he generally kept closed. His chin was deeply dimpled. The complexion was pale, but vital, as is usual with genius.

From a biographical sketch published the year after his death by the Society of the Friends of Music

Schubert's character was simple, confiding and honest. All aglow for art, he was at the same time a loving son, a faithful friend, a grateful pupil. He loved mirth and sociable pleasures; but he ever avoided those circles in which an artist is tolerated only for fashion's sake, and where, constrained by stiff formality, he can never feel at home.

From biographical notes prepared by one of his friends, 1858

Schubert was incredibly fertile and industrious in composing. For everything else that goes by the name of *work*, he had no inclination.

Inscription on Schubert's tombstone, by his friend the poet Grillparzer

The art of music here entombed a rich possession, but even fairer hopes.

—and a comment on the tomb, from a Vienna paper of 6 November 1830
The tombstone is simple—simple as his songs. But it conceals a profound soul, as they do.

Books to read

The fullest reference book is Deutsch's *Schubert: a Documentary Biography* (London 1946). A good, short book is Hutching's *Schubert* (Dent 1945). There are several excellent books on Schubert by Maurice J. E. Brown, and they are highly recommended both for completeness and easiness to read.

There are dozens of books on Schubert. No detail of his life or work is left uncovered. The books mentioned above give the essential facts; after that, the best advice is to browse in a good library, and select for yourself the books that appeal to your own special interest.

Acknowledgements

The authors and publishers would like to thank the following for permission to reproduce illustrations on the pages indicated: Austrian National Tourist Office, 19; Ernst Eulenberg Ltd, 39; Gesellschaft der Musikfreunde, Vienna, 63; Mansell Collection, 11, 37, 55, 67; Museen der Stadt Wien, 52–53; Osterreichische Nationalbibliothek, half title, frontispiece, 2, 29, 30, 40, 44, 49, 51; Radio Times Hulton Picture Library, 5, 7, 14–15, 32, 57, 64. Acknowledgements are also due to J. M. Dent & Sons Ltd for permission to include extracts from *Schubert* by Deutsch and *Schubert* by Hutchings; to Macmillan (London and Basingstoke) Ltd for permission to include extracts from *Essays on Schubert* by Brown; and to George Weidenfeld & Nicolson Ltd for permission to include extracts from *Life in the Vienna of Mozart & Schubert* by Brion.

Important dates: Schubert

1797	31 January Born in Vienna
1808	Becomes chorister at Imperial Seminary
1814	Assistant schoolmaster in his father's school
1817	First published works, including "The Erlking"
1827	Torchbearer at Beethoven's funeral
1828	19 November Dies (aged thirty-one)

Important dates: Others

1732–1809	Haydn
1757–1827	Blake
1770–1827	Beethoven
1792–1868	Rossini
1801	Trevithick's steam engine
1805	Battle of Trafalgar
1805–1849	Johann Strauss I
1809–1847	Mendelssohn
1810–1849	Chopin
1810–1856	Schumann
1811–1886	Liszt
1812–1870	Dickens
1813–1882	Wagner
1815	Battle of Waterloo
1819	Queen Victoria born (ruled England 1837–1901)
1820	Antarctic mainland discovered
1822	Photography invented

Index

Bold figures refer to illustrations